Living in
Italy

ـ th Thomson

ـ ٍ٤ography by David Hampton

FRANKLIN WATTS
LONDON•SYDNEY

PANFORTE MARGHERITA
FIORE
SIENA (Italy)
1827

First published in 2002 by
Franklin Watts,
96 Leonard Street,
London EC2A 4XD

Franklin Watts Australia,
56 O'Riordan Street,
Alexandria, NSW 2015

Copyright © Franklin Watts 2002

Series editor: Ruth Thomson
Series designer: Edward Kinsey

With thanks to Kathryn Britton

A CIP catalogue record for this book is available
from the British Library

Dewey Classification 914.5

ISBN 0 7496 4638 1

Printed in Malaysia

Contents

This is Italy

Italy is one of the easiest countries in the world to recognise on a map. Shaped like a high-heeled boot, it juts into the Mediterranean Sea, in southern Europe. Its pointed toe appears ready to kick Sicily towards Sardinia – two islands which are also part of Italy.

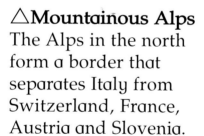

△Mountainous Alps

The Alps in the north form a border that separates Italy from Switzerland, France, Austria and Slovenia.

▷The River Po

Italy's longest river winds through the plain. It provides water for irrigating crops, such as rice, fruit, sunflowers and vegetables.

△The Po valley

A large, low-lying plain, called the Po Valley, lies at the foothills of the Alps. This is the most densely populated and heavily industrialised area in Italy.

Fact Box
Population 57.9 million
Capital Rome
Official language Italian
Main religion Roman Catholic
Highest mountain Mont Blanc (Monte Bianco) 4,807 m
Longest river Po
Biggest cities Milan, Naples, Turin, Palermo, Genoa, Bologna
Currency Euro

SWITZERLAND
AUSTRIA
SLOVENIA
FRANCE

Mt.Blanc
Alps
Lake Como
Lake Maggiore
Lake Garda
● **Milan**
● Venice
● **Turin**
R. Po
Apennines
● Genoa
● **Bologna**
Ravenna ●
● **Carrara**
● Pisa
● Siena
Adriatic Sea
● Rome
SARDINIA
Apennines
● **Naples**
▲ Mt.Vesuvius

Volcanoes

Italy has three
active volcanoes
– Vesuvius, Etna
and Stromboli.

▲ Mt.Stromboli
● **Palermo**
Mt.Etna ▲
SICILY
Mediterranean Sea

▷ Lakes

In the north, there are
long, deep lakes, fed by
the waters of the Alps.
The most famous are
Lake Como, Lake Garda
and Lake Maggiore.

◁ The Apennines

The Apennine
mountains form a
1000 km backbone
down the length of
Italy. In places,
such as Carrara in
the foothills, there
are marble quarries.

▷ The south

The south is far drier,
wilder, less populated
and less visited than
the rest of Italy. It is
an area that suffers
from occasional
earthquakes.

Rome – the capital

Rome is not only the busy capital of modern Italy, but it was once the powerful centre of the ancient Roman empire. Ruins of ancient Rome can be seen all over the city – walls, baths, temples, a racetrack, carved columns, roads and burial vaults, called catacombs.

△The Roman Forum
The Forum was the heart of ancient Rome. People came here to shop, worship in its temples, go to court or do business.

△The Trevi Fountain
Legend has it that visitors who want to come back to Rome must throw a coin over their left shoulder into this fountain.

◁The Colosseum
In ancient Roman times, this massive amphitheatre held 50,000 spectators. They watched gory fights between gladiators, slaves, prisoners and wild animals.

◁ **Saint Peter's Basilica**

Saint Peter's, the biggest church in the world, is in Vatican City. Its huge dome rises above the site where Saint Peter is thought to be buried.

▷ **Swiss Guards**

Vatican City has about 100 Swiss Guards. Their costumes date back to when they were founded in 1506.

▽ **Castel Sant'Angelo**

Originally constructed as a tomb for the Roman Emperor Hadrian, this drum-shaped building was converted into a fortress for the popes. A passageway links it to Vatican City.

Vatican City

The world's smallest country, Vatican City, lies within Rome. It is the headquarters of the Roman Catholic Church, led by the Pope. It has its own passports, coinage, postage stamps, radio station, car number plates and an army of Swiss guards to protect it.

Famous sights

Italy itself is like a museum. Everywhere you go, there is something of interest to see. There are historic old towns, ruined castles, splendid palaces, magnificent cathedrals and churches and hundreds of ancient Roman sites.

Natural wonders

There are also national parks in the mountains, where rare animals, such as the brown bear and wolf, are protected.

◁ **The Leaning Tower of Pisa**
Built on sandy soil, this bell-tower started leaning during its construction in the 13th century. Over the centuries, it has tilted further.

△ **The Galleria in Milan**
This glass-domed arcade of cafes, shops and offices was built nearly 150 years ago. It was one of the first buildings in Europe to be constructed of steel and glass.

△The Grand Canal, Venice
Venice is a unique city, built on over 100 islands, with canals instead of roads. The largest is the Grand Canal, lined with elegant palaces. Tourists can travel along it in unusual-shaped boats, called gondolas.

A poster advertising an exhibition of mosaics

◁Ravenna mosaics
Ravenna's churches are decorated with splendid mosaics. Some date back as far as AD 600.

▽Designer shops
In big Italian cities, there are streets of elegant boutiques selling designer clothes, shoes and jewellery.

Living in cities

More than three-quarters of Italians live in towns or cities. Many towns have an historic centre with narrow, streets and old buildings. The heart of the town is a square (piazza) with a grand palace or church. Some piazzas also have a fountain or the statue of a famous local person.

△ **Car free area**
Cars are banned from most historic centres.

▷ **A piazza**
Piazzas are places to meet and chat.

AREA PEDONALE URBANA

A statue of Garibaldi

◁ **Street names**
Streets are often named after Italian heroes. In 1860, Garibaldi led 1,000 volunteers to free Naples and Sicily from French rule.

△ **The suburbs**
Suburbs have grown up outside larger towns.

▽ **Tourist guides**
Most places produce guides for their many visitors.

▷ **Living in flats**
Most people live in flats. Since they do not have gardens, they often decorate their balconies with flowers and hang their washing out of the windows.

Around town

Days in towns have a particular rhythm. The streets are busy all morning with workers and shoppers. By early afternoon, they are deserted as shops and businesses close for several hours. Lunch is the biggest meal of the day for most Italians.

△ **Town signs**
Illustrated signs point the way to important and useful places.

▷ **Restaurant meals**
Meals are divided into courses. Cold meats or seafood are followed by pasta. The main dish is meat or fish. Vegetables are served separately. Meals end with coffee and dessert.

△ **Travel in town**
Traffic is heavy in most big towns. Special lanes for buses help them move quickly. Many people used mopeds for short journeys.

△**Police (*polizia*)**
Traffic police
make sure that
the traffic keeps
flowing at busy
crossroads.

◁**The *passegiata***
In the late afternoon
and evening, people
come to shop,
people-watch and
meet friends.
Italians call this
evening stroll the
passegiata.

▷**Having a snack**
Stopping for a pastry
and coffee, a sorbet
or an ice-cream is an
essential part of the
passegiata.

Summer days in town
In the hottest months, people often take
a rest in the afternoon. When the day
begins to cool, the shops re-open.
The town centre bustles as people
of all ages come out again.

▷**Opening times**
This sign shows winter
opening hours. During
the summer, some shops
do not re-open until 4 or
5 pm and stay open until
8 or 9 o'clock at night.

13

Living in the country

Far fewer people now live in the country than in the past. Farming has become increasingly large-scale and mechanised, so not as many farm workers are needed to do the work.

△Churches
Every village has a church, often with a tall bell-tower that can be seen for miles around.

▷Villages
Many villages perch on a hill. Some date back to medieval times and had walls built round them for protection.

△Villagers
Villages are increasingly populated by the elderly. Young people who cannot find work in the country move to towns and cities. They often return to their home village at weekends and for holidays.

14

Regional farming

Each region, however, still grows its traditional crops. Farmers whose cows graze on Alpine pastures produce butter and cheese. Those in the Po valley grow wheat and rice or tend fruit orchards. Further south, farmers have olive groves or vineyards.

◁Sunflowers

Sunflowers are an important crop. They are grown for their seeds, which are pressed into oil for cooking.

▷Vineyards

Wine is one of Italy's major exports. Rows of vines cover the sunny hillsides of areas with rich, well-drained soil.

◁Mechanised farming

Farms in the Po valley use big machines to sow and harvest their crops.

Courgette flowers like these are eaten as well as the vegetable itself.

Shopping

There are fewer supermarkets and large department stores in Italy than in many other Western countries. Instead, there is a huge variety of small, specialist shops. Most towns also have a daily or weekly market.

△ **Markets**
Many markets sell clothes and household goods, as well as food.

△ **Food stalls**
Food stalls open only in the mornings, so people can buy fresh fruit and vegetables for lunch, as well as supper.

▷ **A traditional food shop**
A food shop, like this one, sells hams, hard cheeses, preserved and roast meats, olive oil and vinegar, jam, honey, biscuits and other everyday foods.

The baker *(la panetteria)*

The fishmonger *(la pescheria)*

The butcher *(la macelleria)*

A toyshop *(giocattoli)*

△Specialist shops

People buy fresh food from separate shops. There are also individual shops selling hardware, paper and pens, baby clothes or toys.

▷News-stand

Outdoor news-stands sell train schedules and postcards as well as newspapers and magazines.

△ Road signs
Motorways (*autostrada*) are signposted in green. Places of interest are signposted in brown.

On the move

Car ownership in Italy is one of the highest in the world, with one car for every two people. Air pollution has become a big problem in major cities. Some have tried introducing electric cars and car-free days in the city centre.

Motorways criss-cross the country connecting big cities and towns.

Open

Closed

▽ Service stations
Garages are often situated on the outskirts of towns and villages, where there is plenty of space.

◁ Tunnels
Because the country is so mountainous, many road tunnels have been cut through hillsides. Long bridges called viaducts span the valleys on concrete stilts.

△**The metro**
Both Rome and Milan have an underground railway called the metro. The cost of a ticket is the same, however long the journey.

The railway network
Italy has a wide network of railways. Rapid Eurocity trains run between the major cities in Italy and Europe. Fast trains stop at main towns. Slow, local trains stop at every tiny village station.

△**Trains**
Italian trains have a reputation for always leaving and arriving on time.

Train tickets

Family life

Family life is important in Italy. Many Italians live close to their families or, if not, visit as often as possible. Family get-togethers and meals are part of their everyday life.

△Family size
Italians are having fewer children than any other European country. The population is expected to fall in the next ten years.

▷Young and old
It is not uncommon for elderly people to live with their children and grandchildren.

▽TV watching
Almost all Italian families own a TV. Soaps, variety shows and sports are the most popular programmes.

Children at home

Many Italian children enjoy following sport, especially football, playing with Gameboys and Playstations, swapping cards, listening to the latest music, reading comic books and watching videos.

▷ Grandparents

Almost half of all women work, so grandparents often help with looking after children.

▽ Family meals

At weekends, relatives may get together to have a big meal that lasts for several hours.

Time to eat

Italians love good food. Each region has its own distinct dishes, using fresh, locally produced ingredients.

Fresh fish is eaten all along the coast. In the north, people often eat dishes made with beef, rice, potatoes or polenta made from maize.

Spaghetti   Mafaldine

▷ **Pasta**
Pasta is made from wheat. There are more than 200 different shapes.

Penne

Conchiglie

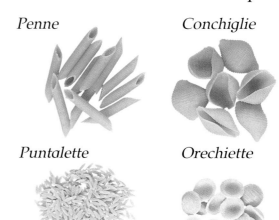

Puntalette

Orechiette

◁ **Breakfast**
Children eat cereal, a piece of fruit or some sweet bread. Many adults have coffee and a pastry in a bar.

▷ **Pizza**
Pizza was created in Naples. It is cooked in a wood-burning oven.

▷Spaghetti

Spaghetti is often eaten with tomato sauce.

▽Italian specialities

Many regional food products, such as these, are exported, as well as being sold in Italy.

Olives

Parma ham

Balsamic vinegar

Pesto – a pasta sauce made from basil

Salami – cured meat

Other cooking styles

In central Italy, people cook with olive oil and eat more pasta, beans and pork specialities, such as ham and salami. In the south, many dishes are based on vegetables and seafood.
In Sicily, food is spiced with chillies. Sicilian cakes and pastries are very sweet and rich.

Panettone – sweet Christmas bread

Pandoro – soft cake

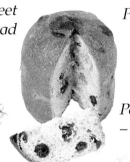

Panforte – fruit cake

Almond pastries

Amaretti – almond biscuits

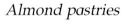

Nutty chocolate

23

School time

Children go to primary school for five years. There are two kinds. Part-time schools have classes six days a week from 8.30 am until 2.30 pm (plus two afternoons). At these schools, children do homework every day. Full-time schools run from 8.30 am until 5 pm every weekday. Children have homework only at weekends.

School bus stop

▷**Getting ready**
At primary school, children wear an overall, called a *grembule*. They take only the books they need for each day and a mid-morning snack, (*la merenda*).

▽**Starting school**
Children start school at the age of six. Those aged between three and five can go to a free full-time nursery school.

24

Secondary schools

At the age of 11, children move to a middle school for three years. Then they choose a secondary school with an emphasis on either classics (Latin, Greek, history and philosophy), science, languages or technical subjects.

Pen with built-in ink eraser

Grammar book

Homework diary

Story writing book

Maths book

◁ Lessons

The main emphasis in primary school is on learning to read and write in Italian. Some children may also start learning English.

Having fun

Italian social life mainly takes place in town squares and streets, especially in warm weather. Friends meet in cafés and restaurants. Children often stay out late for meals with their families.

Spectator sports

Watching football, motor racing and cycle races are Italian national passions.

△**Looking good**
Young Italians are very fashion-conscious. They like to wear designer label clothes and the latest trainers.

There are lots of football magazines.

△▷**Football**
The Italian football League has four main divisions. Series A, the top division, has 18 teams, including AC Milan, Inter Milan and Juventus. They all have their own strips and plenty of merchandise to collect.

Windsurfing in Sardinia

Holidays

Most Italians take their holidays in August, when the weather is too hot and stifling to stay in the cities. Businesses, restaurants and shops in towns close down. Families head for the sea, the mountains or a lake. In winter, many Italians go skiing.

◁ At the lakes
Steamers zigzag up the lakes to places of interest. There are mountain trails for walkers to follow and bathing places for swimmers.

△ At the seaside
Beaches are crowded with foreign tourists, as well as Italians. Some beaches are private and provide umbrellas and loungers, which people pay to use.

Religion

A majority of Italians are Roman Catholic, although fewer and fewer people go to church every Sunday. However, people still celebrate Christmas, Easter Week and important Christian festivals with religious events.

△ Priests
Priests are in charge of the churches. Some still wear long black robes, but others wear modern clothes and even have mobile phones.

▷ All Saints' Day
On 1st November, All Saints' Day, people take flowers to cemeteries to remember their dead relatives.

△ Holy figures
Holy figures, such as the Virgin and Child or a saint, are often painted on old house walls. Sometimes, the figures are carved and stand in niches.

Celebrations

Many places celebrate their local saint's day by carrying his or her statue in a procession around the town.

Costumed festivals

Some towns stage costumed contests each year, with jousting, crossbow, flag-throwing or horse races.

◁ Carnival

In Venice there is a carnival in the ten days up to Lent. People wearing costumes and masks, like these, take over the main square. The festival ends with a masked ball.

▷ The Palio in Siena

The Palio is a horse race held twice a year. After a parade of costumed supporters, riders from different districts of the city race bareback around the Campo (the main square) three times.

COMUNE DI SIENA
PALIO
DEL 2 LUGLIO 1994
FESTIVITÀ DI MARIA SANTISSIMA
IN PROVENZANO

A costumed supporter in the pre-Palio parade

29

Going further

Look for Italian food

Have a look in a supermarket to
see what food it sells from Italy.
How many different sorts of pasta
can you find? What sauces can you
find to go with them? What Italian
cheeses are there?

Make a list of the foods. Notice
whether the labels give the region
that the foods have come from.
Find these regions on a map of
Italy.

Make a city guide

Find out more about one of the
major cities that tourists visit, such
as Venice, Rome, Florence or Siena.

Make a tourist brochure, describing
the city sights, using a piece of
paper folded into three. Draw
some pictures or glue in
photographs cut out from colour
magazines or holiday brochures.
Write short captions about
each sight.

Design a carnival mask

People wear all sorts of
colourful or glittering
masks to the Venice
Carnival. Design your
own Carnival mask. It
could cover either the
whole face or just the
eyes. You may like to
add a fancy hat on to it.

Websites

www.yahooligans.com/Around_the_world/countries/Italy

www.initaly.com

www.enchantedlearning.com/europe/italy

www.cybersleuth-kids.com/sleuth/geography/Europe/Italy

Glossary

Arcade A covered passageway with shops on both sides.

Border The boundary that divides one country from another.

Earthquake A shaking of the Earth, caused by movements of vast plates of rock in the Earth's crust. The most violent earthquakes happen near where the edges of the plates meet.

Exports Goods that are sold by one country to another.

Industrialised Having a large number of industries.

Irrigation System of watering using channels and ditches.

Mechanised Work done using machines.

Medieval From the Middle Ages (the period between the 5th and the 15th centuries).

Merchandise Goods produced which are linked with a 'name', such as a famous football club.

Mosaic Picture or pattern made by fitting together small pieces of marble, glass or ceramic.

Pasture Grassland where animals feed.

Plain An area of flat land.

Population The number of people living in a place.

Quarry A place where rock, stone or slate is cut from an open hillside.

Suburb A district on the edge of a city where people live.

Temple A place of worship.

Vineyards Fields planted with grape vines.

Volcano A cone-shaped mountain lying over a chamber of red-hot, molten rock, called magma. Sometimes pressure from hot gases causes a volcano to erupt.

Index